ART OF THE **MIDWEST** DAVID and AMY *Butler*

BLUE RIBBON

Food
from the
Farm

RECIPES,

HINTS,

and

HOW-TOS

from the

HEARTLAND

farmhand's
Favorite Pies

AMY *and* DAVID BUTLER

with SHARON REISS *and* PHOTOGRAPHY BY COLIN MCGUIRE

SOURCEBOOKS, INC.®
NAPERVILLE, ILLINOIS

Sourcebooks, Inc.

P.O. Box 4410, Naperville, Illinois 60567-4410

(630) 961-3900

FAX: (630) 961-2168

Design by Art of the Midwest Studio

Printed in Belgium

MQ 10 9 8 7 6 5 4 3 2 1

ISBN: 1-57071-677-3

We would like to take this opportunity to thank our friends and editors at MQP for creating this fantastic series and turning us loose on the culinary countryside! To Ljiljana, for keeping our timelines and waistlines in check, and Zaro, for all the inspiration and good faith! To Colin McGuire for lending his keen eye and outstanding vision to convey such flavor through imagery. And special thanks to Sharon Reiss for joining us in this joyful venture. Her passion for the inherent beauty in culinary and all arts and her ability to fill our senses with all the good things in life is the only inspiration we would ever need.

We would also like to thank the farmers, co-ops, and markets which provided us with the fabulous ingredients that make up these fantastic recipes. It *all* starts in the hands of the farmer. And for the untold multitude of country cooks—whose creativity and love invite us home with the sweet aroma of a promise kept warm in the oven—we dedicate this book to you.

CONTENTS

Fair warning. Getting our pies ready!

Culinary Judging today. Building closed until 6:00 P.M.

Pies, like life, take care, nurturing, and attention. An unwatched pie will wander, or in our case, burn. A pie thrown together might have plenty of character, but you wonder about the quality of the ingredients therein and the stability of its shell. Pies can be stiff but yielding, runny and loose, big and fluffy, or thin and flaky. Sound like anybody you know?

And like talented children, you can show off your pies to the family. Offer up a slice and wait for a reaction. Bear in mind that they *are* your family. The same restraint they use on Grandpa when he plays the harmonica, they'll use on your pie if it's "less than heavenly." And so, to really test the capability of your creation, you need to put it out there to be measured against the rest of society. Like sending your gifted child off to public school, or Little League baseball. For pies we have the county fair. No longer protected by the cradling arms of the family (probably thrilled to get *any* pie that they can) your pie goes out into the world to stand on its own, to be counted, and to be judged.

And so the county fair ends up being the center of the pie world. Where all the best rural pies come together and only one walks away with the blue ribbon. Which brings us to this book.

This edition of Blue Ribbon Food from the Farm isn't as much about winning the blue ribbon, as it is about the path leading to it. We spent some time on the farmstead with Sharon, making the pie recipes in this book. We wanted to make sure each one was truly the best of its class. At least that's what the claim was; "research." And what we found was that the farm workers had a thing or two to say on the subject. Of course, they wanted to be a part of the research team (tasters). From a cumulative set of blue ribbon recipes we set about picking one recipe for each famous pie (chocolate cream, key lime, etc.) that captured all the best attributes of that pie, and made the farmhands really happy.

Remember that these are country recipes. Food from the farm. You'll notice that we don't have any chiffon pie recipes and leave out a good many "elaborate" concoctions. We haven't put in any meat pies either. We consider this book to be about American farm favorites. Dessert pies for farmhands and families, reunions and fairs. Not to say that country folks avoid the others, but these are the pies that we're known for and that we're the best at.

You see, America is a cooperative containing a vast array of cultures, even within the farm and rural life. The best part of which is the crossing over of recipes and ideas from region to region. You can imagine the sweet citrus fruits and nuts of the southern gulf plantations and the rich creams and butter of the northern dairy farms, ripened berries and apples from the North Atlantic with fruits and spices from California all meeting together on a wheat farm deep in the hills of the agrarian Midwest. Now we're cooking!

It is this idea of sharing that makes the farm life so rewarding. The idea that knowledge about something good should be passed around and not kept secret, thus enriching the lives of the entire community. That makes everyone happy, which makes you happy. It keeps a smile on the lips of the farmhand—and maybe even the pie judges at the fair.

The art of making a pie is really all about craft. Once you learn the basics of the craft, you can begin to make your own mark upon it. Understand what makes a great filling or pastry and then decide how to make it even better. Pies are not really all that difficult. They just require attention. Getting the pastry right is a big part of creating a perfect pie, and so we've dedicated an entire chapter to that task. We've gathered all the top recipes for you, but we've also pulled together some variations on crusts, toppings, and fillings so that you can create pies in your own image (ha, ha). As we've done in our *Lip Smackin' Jams and Jellies* book, we're introducing some good advice, tips, and a variety of recipes that'll keep you excited about experimenting for a good long time.

So sit back and rifle through these amazing pies. Pick out the ones that speak to your immediate desires. Mark them. Go out and get the freshest ingredients and prepare to set the county fair commissioners and farmhands in your corner of the world on their ears. Or, it could be that pleasing your friends and family is enough. Besides, those little old ladies can get downright vicious when a blue ribbon is at stake.

Oh, did we enter our favorite pies in the county fair? No. It's simple. Sharon is a professional, which isn't fair at the fair! It'd be like sneaking a pro bowler into league night.

Good Bakin'

11

GETTIN' STARTED

EASY AS PIE!

Pie making is so much easier than you may think. There are just a few steps. Making the crust, the filling, and the topping, and putting them all together. Crust making is very simple if you just follow the guidelines laid out in our pastry section. And it's not hard to make a nice, elegant pattern in two-crust pie tops either. Keep in mind that baking will take out the rough edges of many odd cuts and even if it doesn't, that's okay. Great country pies are handmade, rich, and bountiful. They don't pretend to be as "showy" as a cake or frilly pastry. Pies invite you to "dig-in" and partake. Have you ever seen a pie-eating contest? They don't do that for cakes. Pies are judged at the county fair by their relationship with the tongue, not the eye. So let's dig in!

What You'll Need

Clear some space and lay out your necessities:

- *deep pans and bowls for mixing pastries, toppings, and fillings*

- *large wooden spoons and spatulas*

- *pie pans and rings (glass, metal, aluminum, and/or ceramic)*

- *measuring cups and spoons*

- *pastry boards or smooth surfaces for rolling pastry dough*

- *pastry cutter, forks, and knives*

- *rolling pin*

- *mixers, blenders*

- *pie crimper for cutting dough (examples at right)*

- *tart rings and tins—various sizes*

- *fresh ingredients!*

The Foundation—Good Basic Ingredients

Once you've pulled together all the kitchen items you'll need, it's time to go shopping. Here's a rundown on the ingredients and some good advice on them so you can sound well informed when you're talking to the judges at the fair!

Fruits—Choose fruits of each season from your local orchards and fields whenever possible. They will give your recipe that 'local' flavor and will help support area farmers too!

Milk—Unless noted all recipes use whole milk.

Heavy Cream—Contains 36–40 percent fat, which gives it the capacity to be whipped into fluffy toppings. Heavy cream can be frozen, however this alters the fat structure and the cream will not whip. Thawed cream can be used for making fillings, ice cream, and ganache.

Butter—All recipes call for sweet, unsalted, fresh butter. Be certain the brand is A or AA; they contain about 15.5 percent water. Fancy French butters contain even less water so grab them if you can, lesser brands contain more water and this will have an effect on the pastry dough.

Eggs—These recipes use large whole eggs. Try to get to the farmers' market for farm fresh eggs, or use free-range chicken eggs.

Flour—Use bleached all-purpose white flour, without the germ. Sift first and fill the measuring cup pre-sifted spoonfuls. Scrape off top with knife. Because protein contents in flours can vary dramatically use brands such as Pillsbury, King Arthur, or Gold Medal.

Chocolate/Cocoa—Use the very best quality. Ghirardelli and Scharffen Berger are two exceptional American chocolate companies. Use Dutch-processed cocoa for the richest color and tastiest flavored fillings. The best way to keep chocolate and cocoa is in airtight containers at about 60 degrees. (Chocolates will pick up unwanted odors and must not be exposed to dampness.) Dark chocolate will keep for about 2 years under these conditions. White and milk chocolate will hold for about 1 year.

Thickeners—Most fruit pies are thickened with cornstarch, tapioca (processed from the cassava root), or flour. Cream pies are generally thickened with a combination of flour or cornstarch and eggs.

Sugar—Sugar not only gives delicious sweetness to baked goods; it also adds tenderness. Use granulated sugar unless a different kind is specified. If the sugar is lumpy, sift it before using. Brown sugar needs to be rubbed through a sieve if lumpy. To keep brown sugar moist and soft, leave a piece of bread or apple in the sugar jar.

TABLE OF WEIGHTS AND MEASURES

2 teaspoons	1 dessertspoon
3 teaspoons	1 tablespoon
4 tablespoons	¼ cup
8 tablespoons	½ cup
16 tablespoons	1 cup
2 cups	1 pint
4 cups	1 quart
4 quarts	1 gallon
8 quarts	1 peck
Speck, pinch or dash	less than ⅛ teaspoon

●

VARIOUS WEIGHTS

2 cups liquid	1 pound
2 cups shortening	1 pound
¼ lb. print butter	½ cup or 8 tablespoons
4 cups flour	1 pound
1⅞ cups rice	1 pound
2 cups chopped meat (packed)	1 pound

One Crust, Two Crust

On the very base level there are two different types of pies. One crust and two crust. One crust pies are bottom pastry only (with the possibility of a nut, crumb, cream, or meringue top. Two crust pies simply refer to pies with pastry on the bottom and top. But, there are also deep-dish pies (which may have no bottom crust) and tarts (miniature one-crust pies).

So don't be fooled by our chapter headers. They refer to specific aspects of each pie and we prefer to categorize them by their aesthetic rather than their kingdom, phylum, class, genus, or species. Cream pies are really one-crust pies, but cream pies are quite different from buttermilk or pumpkin pies. See what we're getting at?

Remember, Easy as Pie.

When you immerse yourself into piles of flour, butter, eggs, and sugar, remember, this is all in good fun. It's a time to relax and enjoy the creative process. There isn't any inherent pressure in pie-making, only that which you bring upon yourself. A mediocre pie is still better than no pie at all. At least that's what Mom used to say. But it's true. A good pie is the symbol of bounty and reward. It's never been something we've had to make. Unlike breads, meats, and vegetables, it doesn't stand as a staple in our diet. It's good for the soul. Reason enough.

DARN GOOD ADVICE & HINTS

As simple and fun as it all is, there's still some basic advice to follow. You'll want to sterilize your utensils (stick them in boiling water) and keep clean work surfaces. Most of what you'll need to know will be handled in the beginning of each section as the questions that arise tend to be specific to each process, but here is some good starting information about stuff that tends to slip through the cracks!

MAKE LIKE AN EXPERT

Know your ingredients.

Know the roles of your different ingredients, and they will serve you well. Take for instance all-purpose flour—it is specifically formulated for moist, sturdy texture and is quite different from self-rising or bread flours.

★ Use chocolate squares or ½-squares.

Prepare the oven for baking.

Place the racks where the heat is most even, so the pies will bake evenly and brown all around. Always preheat. And don't try to bake too many pies at once or place pans too close to oven walls. Heat must circulate freely inside the oven on all sides. When using more than one rack, stagger the arrangement so that the pies are not on top of each other.

★ Measure shortening by cup, spoon, bar.

Measuring up.

To measure flour. Flour has a tendency to pack on standing, so always sift flour once before measuring. Remember, the cook too busy to bother to sift may put an extra half-cup of flour in their cake and ruin it. Lift the sifted flour lightly by spoonfuls into the measuring cup and level off by drawing the edge of a spatula or straight knife across the top. (Do not press flour or shake it down in the cup.) For fractions of a cup, fill the cup lightly to the proper fraction mark or use graduated cups.

★ Measure sugar level; pack brown sugar.

★ Set the cup level to measure liquid.

To measure shortening. Press shortening into a measuring cup or tablespoon, packing it light-ly. Level off at the top or by the fraction mark in the cup. Butter can be measured as ½ pound for I cup. Shortening can also be measured by water displacement method. For example, to measure ½ cup shortening, fill the cup half full of cold water; add shortening until the water rises to the top. Drain the water!

THE PIE THICKENS

Too much thickener will produce a rubbery filling, and a watery filling results from not enough thickener. Cornstarch used for citrus fillings has a tendency to break down, however, if the fill-ing is cooked and then the lemon juice is added to the cooked filling, it will hold together. Tapioca is best used for fruit pies; it produces a clear, thick filling without covering the taste of the fresh fruit. For lattice pies an extra step is necessary, tapioca sometimes dries out during the baking process and you will have little bits of dried tapioca on top of the fruit. To avoid this, toss ½ of the fruit with the tapioca, fill the pie, and add the balance of the fruit to top the pie.

To keep the filling from curdling, temper the eggs and egg yolks before adding them to cooked cream fillings. To the eggs add a small amount of the hot liquid and mix together. Then add the egg mixture back to the balance of the cooking custard. It is important to bring this mixture to a boil to insure the filling will hold. If you find your filling has a few lumps, pour the hot fill-ing through a fine mesh sieve and the lumps will be gone.

edge flush with the pan lip. Flute the edge of the dough as desired. Cut steam slits. If the pie dough is soft place in the refrigerator for 10–15 minutes before baking. For a lattice or decorative top: a lattice top can be woven loosely or in a tight fashion completely covering the fruit; a decorative top can also be fashioned with a series of punched dots, hearts, or stars. The top piece of dough should be rolled as thinly as possible because when you overlap the top and bottom crust you will double the thickness.

For the lattice you can make it directly on the pie or on a sheet pan and then slide it onto the top of the pie. Roll the dough into an oval shape about 10 inches long. Trim the edges of the dough. With a ruler as a guide, cut the strips of dough with a knife, a pizza cutter, or a pastry cutter; ½" is a good width for the strips. Follow the simple plan on the following pages to create a real "woven" lattice top. Use scissors to trim the edge. Moisten the ends of the strips of dough with water and press down to make them stick to the edge of the bottom crust. Finish border as desired.

Some of the endless varieties of pie top patterns that you can create. Let your imagination run wild, but remember, the pie must be vented in some way to let steam escape.

MAKING LATTICE TOPS

If you know how to weave then you're all set! Follow the visual directions below and you'll see how easy it is to create a "real" woven lattice top pie. We've shown a very simple and large lattice for ease of instruction, but you can create a variety of scales by cutting thin or thick strips. Just follow these basic steps.

A. Lay out strips in a row parallel across the pie top.

B. Pull back every other strip and lay the first cross-strip down at the very edge.

C. Take the pulled strips and lay them back the way they were (over the top of the strip you've just laid down). Now pull back the other strips over the cross-strip and lay down a new cross-strip next to the one you laid before.

D. Repeat this process until the cross-strips go to the edge. Trim excess and finish edge.

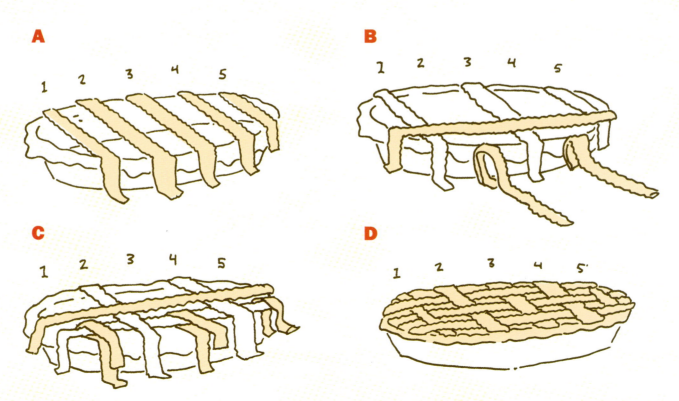

LETTING OFF STEAM

When using a solid top crust for fruit pies, it is very important to make slits or holes in some fashion to vent the steam that builds up during baking. If not, you might just blow your top!

You can make slits in the tops of your crusts after you have placed it over the filling or by first folding the upper crust in half. If you use the folding method, you can make the cuts through both halves of the circle, like cutting a paper doll (shown right).

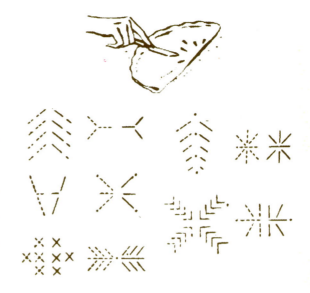

CRIMPING YOUR STYLE

Like a fancy signature, some folks use a specific crimped edge to mark their pies. Shown at the right are a few techniques to make different crimps. When you use a fork, skewer, or metal pie crimper, be sure and dip it in flour first to avoid sticking.

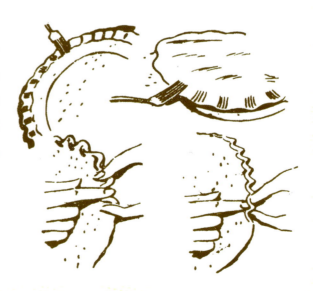

34

BAKING THE CRUST/PIE

A pre-baked pie shell is usually used for cream and glazed fruit pies and tarts. This is done to inhibit the dough from losing its desired shape and puffing during the baking process. To "blind bake" the shell, simply line it with aluminum foil and then fill with dried beans, rice, or pie weights. Place the shell in a preheated, 425-degree oven and bake until the crust is lightly golden brown. Bake for 15–20 minutes (depending on the size of the pie shell it may require more time). Remove the foil after 20 minutes of baking and continue to bake the shell until the dough is dry (about 3–5 minutes).

When baking fruit pies it is best to place a foil-lined sheet pan on a rack below the pie to catch any juices that might find their way outside the pie.

Baking pies from the freezer.

Preheat oven to 425 degrees. Place the frozen pie in the preheated oven and bake for 15 minutes. Lower the temperature to 400 degrees. Bake an additional 25–35 minutes more than the original fresh pie calls for.

How do you know when your pie is done?

The crust of a pie will be tough if it is underbaked. A crust should have an opaque appearance; if the dough looks transparent it is not cooked. The dough contains water and it needs to evaporate. The crust may start to brown unevenly on the surface; however, it may not be cooked inside. The crust can be covered with a piece of foil to reduce undesired browning while the crust is drying out.

Get out your cookie cutters and make some unique pie toppers out of the scrap dough! Follow the guide for the Cinnamon Scraps in this section for preparing them, and then place them on your pumpkin, buttermilk, sweet potato, custard, or other open-top pies!

Good Ol' Never-Fail Pie Dough

Success starts with **INGREDIENTS**

2 ½ CUPS ALL-PURPOSE FLOUR
1 TEASPOON SALT
1 TEASPOON GRANULATED SUGAR
1 CUP UNSALTED BUTTER, CHILLED AND CUT INTO 1" PIECES
4 TABLESPOONS VEGETABLE SHORTENING, CHILLED
3–4 TABLESPOONS ICE COLD WATER

A combination of butter and shortening give this dough a flakier consistency compared to an all-butter crust. Each is equally delicious. This pie dough works very well for double-crusted fruit pies like blueberry or blackberry.

Mix flour and salt together evenly and briskly with a fork or in a food processor. Add butter to the bowl and begin to work the butter into the flour. Add the vegetable shortening, and continue to cut the fat into the flour until it resembles cornmeal. Sprinkle the ice water over the flour mixture and mix several times. Dump the entire mixture into a bowl or onto a working surface and finish incorporating the ingredients together. Do not overwork the dough. Gather the dough into your hands and form a disk of dough, cover with plastic wrap, and chill at least 30 minutes. Roll the dough out on a lightly floured surface to the desired shape and thickness.

Makes 2 8" pie crusts.

Extra-Flaky Pie Dough

Success starts with **INGREDIENTS**

1 ½ CUPS ALL-PURPOSE FLOUR
½ TEASPOON SALT
½ CUP UNSALTED BUTTER, CHILLED AND CUT
    INTO ½" PIECES
3—4 TABLESPOONS ICE WATER

For those who love the flavor of butter, this is the recipe to follow. This dough is great for single-crusted fruit pies and tarts, as well as free-form galettes.

Mix flour and salt together evenly and briskly with a fork or in a food processor. Add butter to the bowl and begin to work the butter into the flour. Continue to cut the fat into the flour until it resembles cornmeal. Sprinkle the ice water over the flour mixture and mix. Dump the entire mixture into a bowl or on a working surface and finish incorporating the ingredients together. Do not overwork the dough. Gather the dough into your hands and form a disk of dough, cover with plastic wrap, and chill at least 30 minutes. Roll the dough out on a lightly-floured surface to the desired shape and thickness.

Makes 1 9—10" pie crust or tart shell.

Super-Flaky Lard Dough

1 ⅓ CUP ALL-PURPOSE FLOUR
¼ TEASPOON SALT
½ CUP LARD, CHILLED
¼ CUP ICE WATER
4 TEASPOONS CIDER VINEGAR

Lard can still be found in the grocery store, usually along with butter and margarine or in the meat department. When working with lard it is important to have it icy cold when making the dough. This will make the dough easier to work with and will keep the dough flaky. Old timers swear by it!

Place flour, salt, and chilled lard in a mixing bowl and blend with a pastry blender or your finger tips until the mixture resembles coarse meal. Mix the ice water and cider vinegar together. Sprinkle the liquid over the dough. Quickly mix together, pull the dough together into a ball, and turn it onto a lightly floured surface. Knead once or twice to keep the dough together. Shape into disks and cover with plastic wrap. Refrigerate for 30 minutes and then use or freeze dough packages.

Dough can be refrigerated for 2 days or frozen for 3 months.

Makes 1 9" pie crust.

Sugar Tart Dough (Paté Sucrée)

2 ½ CUPS ALL-PURPOSE FLOUR
3 TABLESPOONS GRANULATED SUGAR
1 CUP UNSALTED BUTTER, CHILLED AND CUT
   INTO 1" PIECES
4 TABLESPOONS ICE WATER
2 EGG YOLKS, MIXED

This dough is used for tarts. It is sweet and rich, similar to cookie dough. This dough is a little more temperamental than others, because the egg and yolk make it softer. Keep this dough chilled when working with it. It can be made ahead and kept in the refrigerator for 1 day or frozen for 1 month.

In a bowl combine the flour and sugar. Add the butter and process until mixture resembles a coarse meal. Mix together the ice water and egg yolks, add to the dough, and mix until the liquid is absorbed and a ball of dough is formed. This dough will be slightly sticky. Divide dough into two pieces and cover with plastic wrap. Refrigerate for at least two hours, although the dough can be kept in the refrigerator for up to three days.

Makes 2 8–9" tarts.

American Graham Crumb Crust

1½ CUPS FINELY CRUSHED CRUMBS—GRAHAM OR OTHER
2 TABLESPOONS GRANULATED SUGAR
6 TABLESPOONS BUTTER, MELTED
1 TEASPOON OPTIONAL SEASONING, SUCH AS CINNAMON,
    GINGER, COCOA POWDER, OR COFFEE GRANULES

Graham cracker piecrust is an American concept but do not limit yourself to only graham crackers. Try substituting a combination of gingersnaps and walnuts, chocolate wafers, vanilla wafers, shortbread cookies, or amoretti cookies.

Preheat oven to 375 degrees.

In a large bowl, combine all of the ingredients and mix together until the butter is completely absorbed. Dump the mixture into a 9" pie pan and press the mixture as evenly as possible into the bottom and sides of the pan. Place pan in preheated oven and bake for 7–10 minutes or until set and lightly golden in color (chocolate wafers will not show color). Cool the shell before filling.

Makes 1 9" pie crust.

Nutty Crust

1 CUP UNSALTED BUTTER, SOFTENED
¼ CUP GRANULATED SUGAR
¾ CUP FINELY CHOPPED PECANS
1 EGG
1 EGG YOLK
1 TEASPOON SALT
2¾ CUPS ALL-PURPOSE FLOUR

Alternative nuts like almonds or hazelnuts can be substituted for the pecans. This dough is easy to prepare and work with. Unlike pie dough that needs to be rolled and fitted into a pie plate, this dough is pressed into tart pans.

Combine butter, sugar, pecans, whole egg and yolk, and salt in a mixer. Mix only until barely blended. Add flour and mix by hand until all ingredients are incorporated. Wrap the ball of dough in plastic wrap and chill for 4–6 hours. (Dough may be frozen at this point and kept in air-tight packaging in the freezer for up to 1 month.)

Preheat oven to 350 degrees. Press the dough into greased tart pans. The crust should be thick around the edges. Bake empty shells for 12–15 minutes, or until lightly golden brown. Cool. Fill with your favorite custard filling, either plain or topped with fruit.

Makes dough for 8 3" tart pans or 3 8" tart pans.

Cinnamon Scraps

EXTRA DOUGH
CINNAMON SUGAR

Of all the amazing recipes in this book, David's favorite things to eat are these remnants of the pastry making. Great for kids who can't seem to wait until pie eating time (which is rarely right out of the oven). Kids of all ages love them!

Dough scraps can be made into cinnamon cookie strips. Divide the extra dough into strips, place onto greased cookie sheets, and sprinkle with cinnamon sugar. Place in a pre-heated, 425 degree oven and bake until golden brown, about 15–20 minutes. Delicious right out of the oven.

These strips can also be used as a topping for a fruit cobbler (see pages 107–112). Place the unbaked scraps of dough directly onto the prepared fruit filling. Sprinkle the dough with cinnamon sugar or plain sugar and bake at 400 degrees for the specified time.

CREAM PIES

Who can resist the velvety-rich texture and flavor of a cream pie? We can't. This homemade favorite shares top shelf with fruit pies as an American farm classic. A touch fancier than a fruit pie, lighter (great after a big meal), and wonderful right out of the fridge. Where fruit pies beckon to be warmed up and served with coffee on a fall evening, cream pies look to cool you off with a tall lemonade or a big, minty iced tea on a hot summer afternoon.

Most cream pies are a combination of eggs, milk or cream, cornstarch, sugar, salt, and butter, as well as a range of flavors. The eggs or egg yolks help to thicken the cream filling as well as giving it a smooth, satiny texture. Always refrigerate your cream pie after baking!

Very Vanilla Cream Pie

Success starts with **INGREDIENTS**

10 TABLESPOONS SUGAR
4 TABLESPOONS CORNSTARCH
¼ TEASPOON SALT
2 CUPS MILK
½ CUP HALF-AND-HALF
5 LARGE EGG YOLKS, MIXED IN A BOWL
1 TABLESPOON VANILLA EXTRACT

TOPPING:
1½ CUPS HEAVY WHIPPING CREAM
2 TABLESPOONS GRANULATED SUGAR
½ TEASPOON VANILLA EXTRACT

1 CRUMB OR PASTRY SHELL OF YOUR CHOICE

The foundation cream filling for all great cream pies! You can build off of this one.

In a medium saucepan combine sugar, cornstarch, and salt. Add the cold milk and half-and-half. Cook over medium heat, stirring frequently. As soon as the mixture begins to thicken (about 8–10 minutes) remove from the heat. Remove a ¼ cup of the hot milk mixture and add to the egg yolks. Mix. Pour the egg mixture into the hot milk mixture and continue to cook until it comes back to a simmer, constantly stirring. Cook for 1 additional minute. Remove from heat. Add the vanilla. Pour into prepared pie shell. Cover the filling with plastic wrap to prevent a skin from forming. Cool.

Whip the heavy cream with the sugar and vanilla. Spread over the filling and refrigerate until ready.

Makes 1 9"pie.

Banana Velvet Cream Pie

10 TABLESPOONS SUGAR   4 TABLESPOONS CORNSTARCH
¼ TEASPOON SALT   2 CUPS MILK
½ CUP HALF-AND-HALF
5 LARGE EGG YOLKS, MIXED IN A BOWL
1 TABLESPOON VANILLA EXTRACT
1 TABLESPOON RUM
3 LARGE BANANAS

TOPPING:
1½ CUPS HEAVY WHIPPING CREAM
2 TABLESPOONS GRANULATED SUGAR
½ TEASPOON VANILLA EXTRACT

1 CRUMB OR PASTRY SHELL OF YOUR CHOICE

Smooth and light! Great with a crumb crust and our whipped topping.

In a saucepan combine sugar, cornstarch, and salt. Add the cold milk and half-and-half. Cook over medium heat, stirring frequently. As soon as the mixture begins to thicken (about 8–10 minutes) remove from the heat. Remove ¼ cup of the hot milk mixture and add to the egg yolks. Mix. Add the egg mixture to the remaining hot milk mixture and continue to cook until the mixture comes back to a simmer, constantly stirring. Cook for 1 minute. Remove from heat. Add the vanilla. Peel and slice two of the bananas and chop the other. Add the chopped bananas to the custard mixture. Place the sliced bananas in the bottom of the pie shell and pour the custard over them. Cover the filling with plastic wrap. Cool.

Whip the heavy cream with the sugar and vanilla. Spread over the filling and refrigerate until ready. Garnish with banana slices dipped in lemon juice.

Makes 1 9" pie.

Chocolate Heaven Cream Pie

¼ CUP DUTCH-PROCESSED COCOA
3 TABLESPOONS CORNSTARCH
⅔ CUP GRANULATED SUGAR
2 TABLESPOONS UNSALTED BUTTER
1 TABLESPOON VANILLA EXTRACT
4 OUNCES SEMISWEET CHOCOLATE, CHOPPED
2 OUNCES UNSWEETENED CHOCOLATE, CHOPPED

¼ TEASPOON SALT
3 CUPS MILK
2 EGGS

TOPPING:

1 CUP HEAVY WHIPPING CREAM
1 TEASPOON VANILLA EXTRACT

2 TABLESPOONS GRANULATED SUGAR
CHOCOLATE SHAVINGS OR COCOA

1 PIE SHELL, NEVER-FAIL OR EXTRA-FLAKY

The better the quality of chocolate, the better the pie! Truly chocolate heaven.

In a medium-heavy gauge saucepan mix together the cocoa, cornstarch, sugar, salt, and milk. Over medium heat bring mixture to a full boil. Remove from the heat. Add ¼ cup of the hot cocoa mixture to the eggs, mix together, and add back into the saucepan. Cook until mixture returns to a boil, stirring constantly. Remove from the heat and add the chopped chocolates, butter, and vanilla. Whisk until smooth. Pour the mixture through a strainer. Pour into the prepared pan and cover with plastic wrap to prevent a skin from forming. Refrigerate.

Whip the cream with the sugar and vanilla. Spoon over the cooled chocolate filling. Sprinkle the chocolate shavings or cocoa over the whipped cream.

Makes 1 9" pie.

Butterscotch Cream Pie

2 CUPS MILK
3 LARGE EGG YOLKS, BEATEN
3 ½ TABLESPOONS CORNSTARCH
1 CUP DARK BROWN SUGAR
4 TABLESPOONS BUTTER, MELTED
¼ TEASPOON SALT
½ TEASPOON VANILLA EXTRACT

TOPPING:
1 ½ CUPS HEAVY WHIPPING CREAM
2 TABLESPOONS GRANULATED SUGAR
½ TEASPOON VANILLA EXTRACT

1 PIE SHELL, CRUMB OR PASTRY OF YOUR CHOICE

Scalded milk, cornstarch, and dark brown sugar are the secret to this great butterscotch!

Scald the milk in a double boiler. In a medium bowl mix the cornstarch with the brown sugar, and stir in the beaten egg yolks. Add the hot milk gradually, then the butter and salt. Pour into the top of a double boiler and cook until thick. Remove from the heat, cool, and add the vanilla.

Whip the heavy cream with the sugar and vanilla. Spread over the filling and refrigerate until ready to serve.

Makes 1 9" pie.

Note: You can top with the whipped cream recipe above or, for a unique and even sweeter taste, use our meringue recipe!

Ellie's Coconut Cream Dream

10 TABLESPOONS SUGAR
4 TABLESPOONS CORNSTARCH
½ CUP HALF-AND-HALF
5 LARGE EGG YOLKS, MIXED IN A BOWL
1 TABLESPOON VANILLA EXTRACT
1½ CUPS COCONUT, SWEET OR UNSWEETENED

¼ TEASPOON SALT
2 CUPS MILK

TOPPING:
1½ CUPS HEAVY WHIPPING CREAM   ½ TEASPOON VANILLA EXTRACT
2 TABLESPOONS GRANULATED SUGAR

1 PIE SHELL, NEVER-FAIL OR EXTRA-FLAKY

The competition at the fair couldn't pry this recipe away from Ellie, but she liked the idea of her recipe being in a book for everybody else to make! Photo on page 46.

In a pre-heated, 300 degree oven, toast the coconut until light golden brown. Cool. In a medium saucepan combine sugar, cornstarch, and salt. Add the cold milk and half-and-half. Cook over medium heat, stirring frequently. As soon as the mixture begins to thicken (about 8–10 minutes) remove from the heat. Remove ¼ cup of the hot milk mixture and add to the egg yolks. Mix. Add the egg mixture to the rest of the hot milk mixture and continue to cook until the mixture comes back to a simmer, constantly stirring. Cook for 1 additional minute. Remove from heat. Add the vanilla and 1¼ cups of the toasted coconut. Pour into prepared pie shell. Cover the filling with plastic wrap to prevent a skin from forming. Cool.

Whip the heavy cream with the sugar and vanilla, and spread over the filling. Refrigerate until ready. Garnish with additional coconut.

Makes 1 9"pie.

Strawberry Delight Cream Pie

Success starts with **INGREDIENTS**

1 QUART STRAWBERRIES
1 CUP GRANULATED SUGAR
1 CUP COLD WATER
3 TABLESPOONS CORNSTARCH DISSOLVED IN
   ⅓ CUP OF COLD WATER

TOPPING:
1 ½ CUPS HEAVY WHIPPING CREAM
2 TABLESPOONS GRANULATED SUGAR
½ TEASPOON VANILLA EXTRACT

1 SUGAR TART DOUGH CRUST

The cream aspect of this pie comes in the whipped cream! Another traditional way to serve is to put the whipped cream in first, top with berries, and top again with cream.

Select one cup of the strawberries; remove the stems, wash, then place in a pot with the water and one cup of granulated sugar. Boil for 15 to 20 minutes, and then strain through a sieve, crushing the berries with a spoon. When all the juice is squeezed from the berries, throw away the pulp and return the sieved juice to the pot. Gradually add the cornstarch-water mixture, stirring constantly. Bring to a boil. Allow to simmer very slowly until it is a thick syrup. While this is cooking, prepare the rest of the strawberries by washing and removing stems and the white, hard centers. Cut them in halves and pour the syrup over them. Chill. When ready to use, arrange the syrup strawberries in the crust.

Whip the heavy cream with the sugar and vanilla and spread over the filling. Refrigerate until ready.

Makes 1 9"pie.

ONE CRUST FAVORITES

These traditional favorites are open-topped like the cream pies, yet they do not follow the cream pie formula. With fillings that tend to be a bit heavier than cream or fruit pies, we find that there isn't much need for a top to keep it all together—although you'll most likely want to whip up some of our whipped creams to top the peanut butter and pumpkin pies.

Hunker down in the kitchen in the fall and make some of these harvest-time pies, grab a stadium blanket, throw the hay on the wagon, brew some coffee, and set out to picnic in the cool, crisp air. These rich and creamy pies bring the farmhands running.

Perfect Pumpkin Pie

Success starts with **INGREDIENTS**

2 EGGS
¾ CUP SUGAR
1 TEASPOON CINNAMON
½ TEASPOON GINGER
¼ TEASPOON GROUND CLOVES
1 ¾ CUPS PUMPKIN PUREE

½ TEASPOON SALT
1 ⅔ CUPS LIGHT CREAM
OR MILK

TOPPING:
1 ½ CUPS HEAVY WHIPPING CREAM
2 TABLESPOONS GRANULATED SUGAR
½ TEASPOON VANILLA EXTRACT

1 PIE SHELL, NEVER-FAIL OR EXTRA-FLAKY

A classic recipe for a fall favorite. Nothing beats the homemade version!

In a medium bowl mix together eggs, sugar, cinnamon, ginger, cloves, and salt. Whip in pumpkin and add light cream (or milk). Whip until fully blended and thick. Pour into unbaked pie shell and bake at 425 degrees for 15 minutes, then at 350 degrees for about 45 minutes or until inserted knife comes out clean.

Whip the heavy cream with the sugar and vanilla. Spread over the pie after it has cooled and serve.

Makes 1 9" pie.

ONE CRUST FAVORITES

Creamy Cheesecake Pie

1 POUND SOFTENED CREAM CHEESE
1 CUP SUGAR
2 TABLESPOONS FLOUR
2½ CUPS MILK
1 TABLESPOON VANILLA EXTRACT
4 LARGE EGGS, SEPARATED, ROOM TEMPERATURE
JUICE OF ½ LEMON

RASPBERRIES AND CONFECTIONERS' SUGAR FOR TOPPING

2 PIE SHELLS, NEVER-FAIL OR EXTRA-FLAKY

Somehow cheesecake pie seems less dangerous than cheesecake! Wrong. It's decadent.

Preheat oven to 325 degrees. In a large mixing bowl beat at low speed the cream cheese, sugar, and flour until smooth and creamy. Add the vanilla. Continue to beat slowly and add the egg yolks along with the milk. Combine well. Stir in the lemon juice. In a separate bowl, beat the egg whites at high speed with a mixer until soft peaks form. Gently fold the egg whites into the filling mixture.

Divide the filling between the two pie crusts. Bake for 45 minutes, until pies are a golden brown on top and the filling sets. Remove from oven and let cool for at least 1 hour at room temperature. It's best to refrigerate overnight before serving. Prior to serving, add an even layer of raspberries on the top and sprinkle with confectioners' sugar.

Makes two 9" pies.

Dairy Farmer's Buttermilk Pie

Success starts with **INGREDIENTS**

1 ½ CUPS BROWN SUGAR
1 ½ CUPS WHITE SUGAR
1 STICK OF BUTTER
2 TABLESPOONS FLOUR
6 EGGS
½ CUP BUTTERMILK
1 ¼ TEASPOONS VANILLA
½ TEASPOON SALT

2 PIE SHELLS, NEVER-FAIL OR EXTRA-FLAKY

The hands-down favorite of the whole crew! Not too pretty, but simple and sweet!

Cream together the brown and white sugar with the butter. Mix in the flour, buttermilk, vanilla, and salt. Beat in the eggs one at a time. Mix together well. Pour into two unbaked pie shells and bake at 350 degrees for about 30 minutes until the top is a deep golden brown. Do not overbake as it will get watery.

Buttermilk, as country folk know it, is the liquid that remains after the butter has been churned from soured cream. Today we can purchased cultured buttermilk. Its flavor and thickness is not the same as the buttermilk found on the farm of the past, but the flavor of this pie will make you into a buttermilk lover.

Makes 2 9" pies.

Behavin' Peanut Butter Pie

Success starts with **INGREDIENTS**

3 EGGS
1 CUP DARK CORN SYRUP
½ CUP GRANULATED SUGAR
½ CUP CREAMY PEANUT BUTTER
½ TEASPOON VANILLA
1 CUP SALTED PEANUTS, COARSELY CHOPPED

TOPPING:
1 ½ CUPS HEAVY WHIPPING CREAM
2 TABLESPOONS GRANULATED SUGAR
½ TEASPOON VANILLA EXTRACT

1 PIE SHELL, NEVER-FAIL OR EXTRA-FLAKY

There was no misbehavin' close to dinner or we'd miss out on this kid's choice dessert.

Chill an unbaked pie shell.

Beat the eggs and add the corn syrup, sugar, peanut butter, and vanilla. Beat until smooth. Blend the salted peanuts into the mixture. Pour the filling into the chilled, unbaked pie shell and bake for 15 minutes at 400 degrees. Turn down the heat to 350 degrees and bake for an additional 30–35 minutes. Let cool and serve with whipped topping and/or strawberry jam!

Whip the heavy cream with the sugar and vanilla. Spread over the pie after it has cooled and serve.

Makes 1 9" pie.

Franklin Grange Nesselrode Pie

Success starts with INGREDIENTS

1 TABLESPOON UNFLAVORED GELATIN
¼ CUP COLD WATER
2 CUPS LIGHT CREAM OR MILK
2 EGGS, SEPARATED
PINCH OF SALT
¼ CUP AND 6 TABLESPOONS GRANULATED SUGAR
1 ½ TABLESPOON RUM FLAVORING
UNSWEETENED OR SEMISWEET CHOCOLATE SHAVINGS

1 PIE SHELL, NEVER-FAIL OR EXTRA-FLAKY, PRE-BAKED

This is a very old-fashioned recipe for a soothing and rich country sweet pie. It's a bit more complex than cream pies and takes on its own silky texture.

Soak the gelatin in cold water for 5 minutes. Scald the cream in the top of a double boiler. Beat egg yolks with fork; then stir in salt and ¼ cup of sugar. Add scalded cream slowly to the egg yolks, stirring constantly. Return mixture to the double boiler and cook over boiling water, stirring constantly, until smooth and slightly thickened—about 5 minutes. Remove from heat and add gelatin, stirring until dissolved. Pour into a bowl and chill until it begins to thicken. Beat egg whites until quite stiff. Gradually add remaining 6 tablespoons of sugar while beating until it again becomes stiff. Fold into the chilled custard filling along with rum flavoring. Pour into pre-baked pie shell and chill until it has set.

Before serving, garnish with chocolate shavings.

Makes I 9" pie.

AMAZING MERINGUE!

Stick with fresh ingredients in a simple recipe and a mountain of meringue can be made! We've put in a few pointers for you since, while meringue is fairly easy to make, it can be tricky to get just right. Usually the pies that lie underneath are tart and tangy to compliment the cool, sweet, and smooth texture of a tall meringue. Use this topping for other fruit pies as well to mix up your repertoire of pie surprises!

Sugar, egg whites, and a little bit of vanilla is all that is needed. They make it seem so fancy in the restaurants!

Stable Meringue Topping

This is a favorite American topping, with mounds of whipped egg whites and sugar browned to a golden color in the oven. Meringue can be temperamental, however, so here are some hints to make your meringue topping look like a mountain top.

Meringue often fails—not due to humid weather—but because it is not cooked properly. When making a meringue-topped pie, prepare the filling and keep it warm while you make the topping. Spoon the meringue topping over the warm pie filling. The filling has to be warm to allow the meringue to cook thoroughly. A sprinkle of fine cake crumbs between the hot filling and meringue can also keep the filling from weeping. The meringue will also weep if the sugar is not dissolved properly during the beating process. Gradually add sugar to the egg whites to allow the sugar to dissolve, about a tablespoon at a time. The ratio of sugar to egg white is crucial, use 1 tablespoon sugar per egg white. A small amount of cream of tartar will add stability to the meringue.

- *Eggs separate best when they are cold; the whites must be clean, with no yolk attached.*
- *Overbeaten egg whites will collapse. To revive them, beat 1 egg white until frothy, then carefully fold into the beaten egg white mixture.*

½ CUP SUPERFINE SUGAR
2 TABLESPOONS WATER
½ CUP EGG WHITES—ABOUT 4 LARGE EGG WHITES
½ TEASPOON CREAM OF TARTAR

In a medium saucepan mix together the sugar and the water. Cook over medium heat stirring constantly, until sugar is dissolved and bubbling. Turn heat to lowest setting and stop stirring. Using a mixer, beat the egg whites until foamy. Add the cream of tartar and continue to beat until stiff peaks form. Check the temperature on the sugar syrup; it should read 236 degrees (soft ball stage). Pour the sugar syrup into the egg whites steadily. Beat at high speed for 2 minutes. Scrape the bowl and beat an additional minute. Spoon the mixture on top of the warm pie filling. Bake the pie in a pre-heated, 350 degree oven for 12–15 minutes, or until the meringue is golden brown.

Tangy Lemon Meringue Pie

8 EGGS, SEPARATED
½ CUP PLUS 1 TABLESPOON CORNSTARCH
1 ⅓ CUP GRANULATED SUGAR
2 ½ CUPS WATER
1 TABLESPOON GRATED LEMON ZEST
1 ½ CUP LEMON JUICE, FRESHLY SQUEEZED
PINCH OF SALT
3 TABLESPOONS UNSALTED BUTTER

1 PIE SHELL, NEVER-FAIL OR EXTRA-FLAKY, PRE-BAKED
1 BATCH STABLE MERINGUE TOPPING

Tart meets sweet in this classic combo. Pile high your meringue and serve chilled.

Place egg yolks in a separate bowl and set aside. In a medium, nonreactive (do not use aluminum) saucepan, whisk together the cornstarch, sugar, and water. Cook over medium heat until thick, smooth, and translucent. Temper the egg yolks with some of the hot mixture and add the yolk mixture to the saucepan. Whisk until incorporated and remove from heat. Add salt, zest, lemon juice, and butter, and mix until smooth. Pour into a baked pie shell. Cover with plastic wrap to keep a skin from forming and to keep the filling warm while you prepare the meringue topping.

Make the meringue following the recipe on page 68. Spoon the mixture on top of the warm pie filling. Bake the pie in a pre-heated, 350 degree oven for 12–15 minutes, or until the meringue is golden brown.

Makes 1 9" pie.

Orange Silk Meringue Pie

1 CUP GRANULATED SUGAR
2 TABLESPOONS CORNSTARCH
3 EGGS, SEPARATED
1½ CUPS FRESH-SQUEEZED ORANGE JUICE, STRAINED
2 TEASPOONS GRATED ORANGE ZEST
⅛ TEASPOON SALT
2 TABLESPOONS UNSALTED BUTTER

1 PIE SHELL, NEVER-FAIL OR EXTRA-FLAKY, PRE-BAKED
1 BATCH STABLE MERINGUE TOPPING

A sweet citrus pie that's not as tart as the lemon but every bit as good!

In the top of a double boiler mix together the sugar, cornstarch, egg yolks, orange juice, zest, salt, and butter. Mix over hot water until the mixture is thick and creamy. Pour the filling into the prepared pie shell. Cover with plastic wrap to keep a skin from forming and to keep the filling warm while you prepare the meringue topping.

Make the meringue following the recipe on page 68. Spoon the mixture on top of the warm pie filling. Bake the pie in a pre-heated, 350 degree oven for 12—15 minutes, or until the meringue is golden brown.

Makes 1 9" pie.

FRUIT PIES

Fruit pies stand as a tribute to the hard work and bounty of harvest. They are a reward for good work. They are as rich as the land is enriching. You just can't beat 'em.

The American apple pie is the perfect country food. It encompasses all the positive aspects of warmth, nurturing, and sweetness that define farm life. But choosing the right variety of apple for your pie can be a real chore. Here's a short primer for you: fall pies can be made with Wealthy, Cortland, and Stayman-Winesap apples. These varieties are found at roadside markets or local orchards. Some people prefer the green, tart varieties such as the Lodi or Rhode Island Greening apples. Pie apples that are available year round and around the country are Golden Delicious, Newtown, and Pippin. In the middle of winter, use a combination of apples such as sweet Golden Delicious and tangy Granny Smith apples. For variations, substitute 1 cup of cranberries or blackberries for a cup of apples.

Blue Ribbon Apple Pie

Success starts with **INGREDIENTS**

7 CUPS APPLES, SLICED THINLY
2 TABLESPOONS UNSALTED BUTTER
½ CUP GRANULATED SUGAR
½ CUP LIGHT BROWN SUGAR
1 TABLESPOON LEMON JUICE
1 TEASPOON CINNAMON
PINCH OF NUTMEG
1 TABLESPOON CORNSTARCH

1 PIE SHELL, NEVER-FAIL OR EXTRA-FLAKY

The one recipe to pass down the line. Although the lattice top gives this pie a charming and dramatic appearance, it is still a double-crusted pie. Refer to page 32 for instructions on assembling a lattice top.

(Note: for this recipe the filling should be prepared before rolling the pastry dough.)

In a skillet over high heat, melt the butter, quickly add the apples, and sprinkle with ¼ cup of granulated sugar. Sauté the apples until just soft; do not overcook. Drain the apples in a colander and cool. Mix together the remaining ¼ cup of granulated sugar, brown sugar, lemon juice, cinnamon, nutmeg, and cornstarch. Toss with the cooked apples. Place apple mixture into the pie pan lined with pastry dough. Roll remaining piece of pie dough and assemble a lattice or simply roll dough to fit the pie pan. Cover the filling. Trim edges and seal with the bottom pastry edge. Crimp the edges to seal. Brush dough with cream and sprinkle with sugar. Cut 2–4 vents for steam (if using a solid top). Bake in a preheated 450 degree oven for 10 minutes. Lower temperature to 350 degrees and continue to bake for 40 minutes longer, or until the crust is golden brown. Remove pie from oven and cool to room temperature before serving.

Makes 1 9" pie. *Serve with cheddar cheese or vanilla ice cream.*

Dig-Down Deep-Dish Apple Pie

Success starts with **INGREDIENTS**

6 LARGE MCINTOSH APPLES, PEELED, CORED, AND CUT INTO 1" PIECES [8 CUPS]

1 CUP SOUR CREAM
1 LARGE EGG
2 TEASPOON VANILLA

¾ CUP GRANULATED SUGAR
⅓ CUP ALL-PURPOSE FLOUR
½ TEASPOON SALT

CRUMBLE TOPPING:
1 CUP WALNUTS, CHOPPED
⅓ CUP GRANULATED SUGAR
⅓ CUP BROWN SUGAR
8 TABLESPOONS UNSALTED BUTTER, SOFTENED

½ CUP ALL-PURPOSE FLOUR
1 TABLESPOON GROUND CINNAMON

1 DEEP-DISH PIE SHELL, UNBAKED, USE THE NEVER-FAIL RECIPE, BUT SUBSTITUTE COLD APPLE CIDER OR JUICE FOR ICE WATER

For the apple filling, put all the ingredients in a large mixing bowl and toss together. Spoon mixture into the prepared pie shell and bake in a pre-heated, 450 degree oven for 10 minutes. Reduce heat to 350 degrees and bake an additional 35 minutes.

For the crumble topping, put all ingredients in a large bowl and work with your hands until the mixture is crumbly. Do not overmix and work it into a paste. (If this happens place the mixture in the refrigerator and chill. Break the chilled mixture into bits.)

Remove pie from oven and crumble the streusel topping on the apples.
Return to the oven and bake an additional 15 minutes at 350 degrees.

Makes 1 9" pie.

Deep-Dish Peach Pie

Success starts with **INGREDIENTS**

2 POUNDS PEELED PEACHES [6 CUPS]
1 CUP OF JUICE DRAINED FROM THE PEELED PEACHES
¾ CUP GRANULATED SUGAR
2 TABLESPOONS QUICK-COOKING TAPIOCA
½ TEASPOON CINNAMON, GINGER,
    OR NUTMEG, OPTIONAL

1 DEEP-DISH PIE SHELL, NEVER-FAIL RECIPE

In the summer, when nectarines and apricots are equally delicious as peaches, make substitutions or combine the stone fruits for a change. The technique for this pie may seem odd at first, however, it all comes together very quickly.

Peel peaches, then drain to catch all of the released juices. If you have less than 1 cup, add water or apple juice. In a large nonstick fry pan, combine the fruit juice, sugar, spice, and tapioca. Mix. Add the fruit, and let it rest for 15 minutes (the tapioca needs to soften). Over medium heat, bring the mixture to a boil. Simmer the peaches until tender and the sauce thickens, but the peaches should hold their shape.

Spoon mixture into the prepared pie shell. Assemble a lattice or simply roll a piece of dough to fit the pie pan. Cover the filling. Trim edges and seal with the bottom pastry edge. Crimp the edges to seal. Brush dough with cream and sprinkle with sugar. Cut 2–4 vents for steam (if using a solid top). Place pie shell in a pre-heated, 450 degree oven for 10 minutes. Reduce heat to 350 degrees, and bake an additional 35 minutes.

Makes 1 9" pie.

Town's Diner Cherry Pie

4 CUPS FRESH, PITTED SOUR CHERRIES
1 ¼ CUPS SUGAR
4 TABLESPOONS FLOUR
2 TEASPOONS QUICK-COOKING TAPIOCA
1 TABLESPOON LEMON JUICE
1 DROP ALMOND FLAVORING
1 TABLESPOON BUTTER

1 PIE SHELL, NEVER-FAIL, EXTRA-FLAKY, OR SUPER-FLAKY LARD DOUGH

A truck stop staple. This cherry pie is the standard that brings 'em back home.

Preheat oven to 450 degrees.

Place the cherries in a large mixing bowl. In a different bowl, combine the sugar, flour, tapioca, lemon juice, and almond flavoring. Mix well and sprinkle over the cherries, stirring gently until well blended. Pour into unbaked 9" pie shell with dough of your choice. Cover as a solid top (shown at the beginning of this section with circles cut into it) or a lattice top. Be sure to vent solid top! Bake at 450 degrees for 10 minutes, and then reduce heat to 350 degrees and continue to bake for about 35–40 more minutes.

Makes 1 9" pie.

Blue-Razz Berry Pie

Success starts with **INGREDIENTS**

4 CUPS FRESH BLUEBERRIES

4 CUPS FRESH RASPBERRIES

[NOTE: IF USING FROZEN BERRIES, MEASURE FROZEN THEN THAW BEFORE FILLING THE PIE; TAPIOCA NEEDS TO DISSOLVE IN JUICES.]

¾ CUP GRANULATED SUGAR

3 TABLESPOONS QUICK-COOKING TAPIOCA

1 TABLESPOON FRESH LEMON JUICE

¼ TEASPOON CINNAMON

1 PIE SHELL, NEVER-FAIL, EXTRA-FLAKY, OR SUPER-FLAKY LARD DOUGH

This recipe can be used for any small, dark berries. Just keep to 8 cups of berries. Use all the same kind of berry if you choose. Blackberry is another favorite!

Preheat oven to 400 degrees.

On a lightly floured surface roll out one piece of dough to line the bottom of the pie pan, allow 1 inch of dough to drape over the pie rim. Chill.

For the filling, mix all ingredients together. Fold several times to allow juices from the berries to be released. Allow filling to sit for 15 minutes (tapioca needs time to dissolve). Spoon berry mixture into the lined pie pan. Roll out the remaining piece of dough. Place the dough over the berries and crimp the edges with your fingers or with a fork. (You can also choose to cover this pie with a lattice top.) Brush the top of the pie with water and sprinkle with sugar. Bake at 400 degrees for 15 minutes; then reduce heat to 350 degrees. Bake an additional 35 minutes, or until juices begin to bubble. Remove pie from oven and cool before serving.

Makes 1 9" pie.

Pucker-up Rhubarb Pie

 *Success starts with* **INGREDIENTS**

4 CUPS FRESH RHUBARB, CUT IN SMALL CUBES
½ TEASPOON CINNAMON
5 TABLESPOONS FLOUR
¼ TEASPOON GRATED LEMON RIND
⅓ TEASPOON GRATED ORANGE RIND
⅛ TEASPOON SALT
2 CUPS SUGAR
3 TABLESPOONS BUTTER, MELTED
3 EGGS, LIGHTLY BEATEN

1 PIE SHELL, NEVER-FAIL, EXTRA-FLAKY, OR SUPER-FLAKY LARD DOUGH

Tart enough for ya? A classic for the town gardener as it doesn't take much rhubarb to make a fine pie. Great for quieting gossipy relatives.

Preheat oven to 450 degrees.

On a lightly floured surface roll out one piece of dough to line the bottom of the pie pan, allow 1 inch of dough to drape over the pie rim. Trim the edges. Partially bake the crust for 10–12 minutes at 450 degrees. Remove and cool. Turn oven to 400 degrees.

In a large bowl combine the rhubarb, cinnamon, flour, lemon rind, orange rind, salt, sugar, and butter. Mix well and let set for a few minutes. Put into the partially baked pie shell. Pour the lightly beaten eggs over the filling. Top the pie with lattice or a well-ventilated solid top. Brush with cream and sprinkle with sugar. Bake for 15 minutes at 400 degrees, and then turn down to 350 degrees and bake for 45 minutes more.

Makes 1 9" pie.

Sweet Concord Grape Pie

Success starts with **INGREDIENTS**

4 CUPS CONCORD GRAPES
1 CUP SUGAR
⅛ TEASPOON SALT
1 ½ TABLESPOONS QUICK-COOKING TAPIOCA
⅛ TEASPOON CLOVES

1 PIE SHELL, NEVER-FAIL, EXTRA-FLAKY, OR SUPER-FLAKY LARD DOUGH

A summer fruit pie that even tastes great chilled. Guaranteed to summon "ooh's and aah's" from your kinfolk.

On a lightly floured surface roll out one piece of dough to line the bottom of the pie pan, allow 1 inch of dough to drape over the pie rim. Chill.

Slip grapes from their skins. Steam pulp in double boiler for 20 minutes. Press through coarse sieve to remove seeds. Add strained pulp to skins. Combine sugar, salt, tapioca, and cloves; add to grapes. Let stand for 15 minutes. Preheat oven to 400 degrees. Spoon grape mixture into the lined pie pan. Roll out the remaining piece of dough. Place the dough over the grapes and crimp the edges with your fingers or with a fork. (You can also choose to cover this with a lattice top.) Brush the top of the pie with water and sprinkle with sugar. Bake at 400 degrees for 15 minutes; then reduce heat to 350 degrees. Bake an additional 35 minutes, or until juices begin to bubble. Remove pie from oven and cool before serving.

Makes 1 9" pie.

SOUTHERN FAVORITES

Southerners know sweet. They talk sweet, they smile sweet, and they even make their iced tea sweet. If there's anything a Yankee farm boy loves, it is to travel south and have a taste of anything made of pecans, sweet potatoes, limes, or custard! They're just rollin' in it down there.

So we wouldn't have dreamed of finding any of the following recipes north of the Mason-Dixon line. Instead, we went down south to find the blue ribbon recipes there. And to "wash down" our pies, we had plenty of sweet tea and grits, and some pralines and fried chicken, too!

I'm thinking maybe we should have jogged back to Ohio.

S'uthun Supreme Pecan Pie

Success starts with **INGREDIENTS**

3 EGGS
2 TABLESPOONS BUTTER, MELTED
2 TABLESPOONS FLOUR
½ TEASPOON VANILLA EXTRACT
⅓ TEASPOON SALT
½ CUP SUGAR
1 ½ CUPS MAPLE SYRUP
1 ½ CUPS BROKEN PECAN HALVES
1 CUP HALVED PECANS

1 PIE SHELL, EXTRA-FLAKY OR SUPER-FLAKY LARD DOUGH

Ya'll might have a hard time keeping this pie around. Best to double it!

Preheat oven to 425 degrees.
On a lightly floured surface roll out one piece of dough to line the bottom of a 9" pie pan, allow 1 inch of dough to drape over the pie rim. Cut off excess and crimp pie edge as you see fit. In a mixing bowl, beat the eggs until light. Blend in the melted butter, flour, vanilla extract, salt, sugar, and maple syrup. Sprinkle the broken pecans over the bottom of the pie shell. Gently pour the mixture in, and then make rings of pecan halves, starting from the middle and working out until the surface is covered. Bake at 425 degrees for 10 minutes and then reduce heat to 325 degrees and continue baking for about 40 minutes. Let cool before serving.

Makes 1 9" pie.

Alabama Sweet Potato Pie

Success starts with **INGREDIENTS**

2 CUPS MASHED AND SIEVED SWEET POTATOES
1 CUP GRANULATED SUGAR
½ TEASPOON GROUND CINNAMON
½ TEASPOON GRATED NUTMEG
½ TEASPOON SALT
2 LARGE EGGS, SEPARATED
2 TEASPOON VANILLA EXTRACT
⅔ CUP UNSALTED BUTTER, MELTED
1 ½ CUP MILK, ROOM TEMPERATURE

2 PIE SHELLS, EXTRA-FLAKY OR SUPER-FLAKY
LARD DOUGH

Pictured at the beginning of this section. A little slice of heaven!

Preheat the oven to 350 degrees.
On a lightly floured surface roll out the dough to line the bottoms of two 9" pie pans, allow 1 inch of dough to drape over the pie rims. Cut off excess and crimp pie edges as you see fit.

In a mixing bowl combine all the ingredients except the egg whites. Mix thoroughly. In a clean bowl beat the egg whites until they are frothy and hold a soft peak. Fold into the potato mixture. Pour the filling into the prepared pie shells. No crust tops needed! Bake for 40–45 minutes.

Is great topped with whipped cream and pecans!

Makes 2 9" pies.

Alice's Smooth Vinegar Pie

1 EGG, BEATEN
3 TABLESPOONS CIDER VINEGAR
1 TEASPOON LEMON EXTRACT
4 TABLESPOONS ALL-PURPOSE FLOUR
1 CUP SUGAR
1 CUP BOILING WATER

TOPPING:
1½ CUPS HEAVY WHIPPING CREAM
2 TABLESPOONS GRANULATED SUGAR
½ TEASPOON VANILLA EXTRACT

1 PIE SHELL, EXTRA-FLAKY OR SUPER-FLAKY LARD
DOUGH, PRE-BAKED

A mild and lightly sweet pie that makes for a great summer afternoon treat.

Prebake your pie shell (see page 35).

Mix sugar and flour together in a saucepan. Add boiling water. Cook for 5 minutes on medium heat, stirring. Add the beaten egg and cook for two more minutes, stirring. Add the lemon and vinegar. Cook for a few more minutes, stirring well. Pour into pre-baked pie shell and let cool.

Whip the heavy cream with the sugar and vanilla, and serve alongside pie and a dollop beside each pie slice.

Makes 1 9" pie.

Ol' General's Custard Pie

Success starts with **INGREDIENTS**

1 CUP BUTTER
2 CUPS GRANULATED SUGAR
5 EGGS, SEPARATED
½ TEASPOON VANILLA EXTRACT

ADDL. ⅓ CUP SUGAR FOR EZ MERINGUE TOPPING

1 PIE SHELL, EXTRA-FLAKY OR SUPER-FLAKY LARD DOUGH

Custard pies are a delicate treat. They're also contrary, because they combine two kinds of foods that bake at entirely different temperatures: custard and crust. Custard cooks at lower temperatures, so chilling it before the baking is very important!

Cream the butter until soft and smooth; add the 2 cups sugar gradually and blend it well. Add the egg yolks to this and beat well. Beat 2 egg whites with the salt and vanilla until stiff. Fold egg whites into the butter mixture. Chill this mixture for 30–60 minutes.

Preheat oven to 425 degrees.

When ready to bake, pour cool mixture into unbaked pie shell, and bake for 12 minutes. Then decrease heat to 300 degrees and bake for about 20 minutes longer. When you remove the pie from the oven, turn oven to 350 degrees.

Beat the three remaining egg whites until stiff. Gradually add the 1/3 cup sugar, and beat until thick and smooth. Pile meringue on top of hot filling, being sure to touch edge of pastry all around. Bake at 350 degrees for 12–15 minutes, until meringue is delicately browned.

Makes 1 9" pie.

Classic Key Lime Pie

21 OUNCES SWEETENED CONDENSED MILK
6 EGG YOLKS
1 CUP FRESH LIME JUICE
1 TABLESPOON GRATED LIME ZEST

1 AMERICAN GRAHAM CRACKER CRUST

Key limes aren't always around (especially up north) so we use regular, fresh limes for this recipe. Taste the filling as you go to decide on how tangy you'd like it.

Preheat oven to 325 degrees.

Press graham cracker crust into the bottom of a 9" glass pie dish. Bake for 10 minutes, remove from heat, and let cool for at least 10 minutes.

In a medium-sized bowl, on the low speed of your electric mixer, beat the milk, yolks, and lime juice. Taste it to see if it's tart enough. If not, add a bit more lime juice! Add the lime zest and mix. Carefully pour into the cooled pie crust. Bake for 25–30 minutes, or until the middle has set. Allow to cool for 20 minutes. Sprinkle with lime zest and garnish with sliced lime before serving.

You can also add our meringue recipe for the perfect topper!

Makes 1 9" pie.

HANDMADE RUSTIC TARTS

A great way to get your pie bakin' feet wet or create some amazing one-of-a-kind treats for a multitude of tastes! The character and charm of these recipes lie in the fact that they are made to be eaten, not studied. Pack them with all the good things in life and wrap 'em up.

A tart is an open-face, filled pastry shell; it is either baked and removed from fluted tart pans or prepared in flan ring forms and served. Another type of tart, a galette or croustade, is baked in a free-form style. Tatins are also popular and are generally prepared with apples or pears. Tarts are easier to serve than pies because they are presented without the pan and cutting them is much easier. Tarts come in all shapes and sizes. Nut doughs, sugar doughs, and cream doughs work well for tart shells.

Caramelized Pear Tatin

1 RECIPE NEVER-FAIL PIE DOUGH, ROLLED INTO AN
11 INCH CIRCLE, CHILLED

3 POUNDS BOSC PEARS, PEELED, HALVED AND CORED
JUICE FROM 1 LEMON
½ CUP GRANULATED SUGAR
¼ CUP WATER
4 TABLESPOONS UNSALTED BUTTER, CUT INTO BITS

Nothing can be better than a warm pear tart fresh from the oven to finish a dinner in autumn or winter. The pears can be cooked and cooled and a piece of pie dough can be draped over the top of the cooled pears, covered with plastic wrap, and placed in the refrigerator for several hours before baking.

Rub each pear half with a little lemon juice. In a 9-inch, cast-iron pan or a non-stick skillet melt the sugar with the water and cook until it caramelizes. Arrange the pears cut side up in the hot caramel. Fit the pears in tightly. Cook over medium heat for 10–15 minutes, basting with the juices. The fruit should be just tender. Do not overcook or the pears will turn to mush when they are baked. Cool. To finish the tatin, preheat oven to 425 degrees for 30 minutes. Dot the pears with the butter, place the rolled pastry dough on top of the cooled pears and tuck in the edges of pastry dough inside the pan. Cut 2 vents into the pastry. Place tart in the center of the oven and bake for 30 minutes or until pastry is golden brown. Cool tart 10 minutes. To unmold, place a plate or cutting board on top of the pan and invert. Be careful—some of the juices will escape and the syrup will be hot. Serve warm.

Makes 1 9" free-form tart.

Apple Galette

Success starts with **INGREDIENTS**

1 RECIPE OF EXTRA FLAKY DOUGH MADE WITH ALL
    BUTTER, AS THE TART NEEDS TO BE STURDY
4–5 LARGE APPLES—GOLDEN DELICIOUS, PIPPIN,
    OR GRANNY SMITH, PEELED, CORED, SLICED THINLY
2 TABLESPOONS UNSALTED BUTTER, CUT INTO ½" BITS
⅓ CUP SUGAR
½ CUP APRICOT PRESERVES, STRAINED,
    MIX IN 1 TABLESPOON OF COGNAC

Galettes are prepared in a free-form style and have a rustic country look. They are perfect to tote along to picnics or serve at a dinner buffet. The baked fruit filling is generally glazed to give the tart some additional flavor and make it glisten.

Preheat oven to 400 degrees. Roll chilled pastry dough into a circular shape about ¼" thick. Place the dough onto a cookie sheet. Arrange the sliced fruit in diagonal rows on the dough, overlapping to simulate tiles on a roof. Leave a 1½" border of dough around the fruit filling. Fold the border back onto the fruit. The edges will not look perfect. If the dough is soft, place the tart in the refrigerator for 30 minutes before baking. Dot the top of the fruit with small bits of dough and sprinkle with the sugar. Bake for 40–50 minutes. Cool slightly and paint the fruit with warm glaze. Cut into wedges and serve with ice cream.

Other Great Galettes:
Mixed Berry: Use 3 cups of mixed berries for the apples and a currant jelly glaze.
Stone fruit: Use 3 cups of a combination of fresh apricots, peaches, and plums, and a currant jelly glaze.
Fall Harvest: Use 3 cups of sliced pears, apples, walnuts, raisin, dried apricots, and cinnamon and apricot preserves for the glaze.

Fresh Fruit Tart

Success starts with **INGREDIENTS**

1 RECIPE SUGAR TART DOUGH OR NUTTY CRUST
FRESH FRUIT OF YOUR CHOICE

PASTRY CREAM FILLING:

2 CUPS WHOLE MILK
½ VANILLA BEAN, SPLIT
⅔ CUP GRANULATED SUGAR
¼ CUP CORNSTARCH
4 EGG YOLKS

1 WHOLE EGG
2 TABLESPOONS UNSALTED BUTTER
2 TEASPOONS VANILLA EXTRACT

You can use any fruit that takes your fancy in this one. Try a medley of berries, fresh fall apples, or juicy pears. Top it all off with rich, toothsome pastry cream.

To make the pastry cream, warm 1½ cups milk in a saucepan. Remove from heat. Place vanilla bean in milk, cover, and allow to infuse for 15 minutes. Remove bean. Add sugar and stir to dissolve. Place over medium heat and bring to a boil. In a separate bowl combine the remaining milk, cornstarch, egg yolks, and the egg, and whisk. Temper this with ½ cup of the hot milk mixture. Pour back into the saucepan and whisk. Return to a boil and cook for a minute, whisking. Do not let it scorch. Remove from heat and whisk in the butter and vanilla extract. Mix. Sieve into a bowl. Cover with plastic wrap.

Roll dough out to a circle ¼" thick. Gently press into a tart pan. Trim by rolling the top of the tart pan with a rolling pin. Refrigerate for at least 30 minutes. Preheat oven to 400 degrees. Prepare the shells for blind baking (see page 35). Bake the lined shell for 8 minutes. Remove the foil liner and bake the empty shell for a few more minutes, or until the pastry is a light golden brown. Cool. Remove the baked pastry from the tart pan. To finish the tart, fill with some pastry cream and decorate the top with fruit and glaze.

Baked Apricot Tart

 *Success starts with* **INGREDIENTS**

1 RECIPE SUGAR TART DOUGH
3 CUPS FRESH APRICOTS, HALVED AND PITTED
ABOUT 1 ½ POUNDS
4 TABLESPOONS SUGAR
6 TABLESPOONS APRICOT JAM

A fantastic foundation for the juiciest apricots! Serve with an abundance of ice cream.

Roll the pastry dough and transfer dough to a rectangular tart pan or an 8" pie plate. Preheat oven to 400 degrees.

Spread 6 tablespoons apricot jam into the bottom of the tart pan. Place the halved apricots on top and sprinkle with sugar. Bake the tart for 30–35 minutes, until the crust is golden brown and the apricots begin to caramelize. The apricots should be bubbly. Cool the tart on a rack. Dust the baked tart with powdered sugar. Serve at room temperature.

Makes 1 tart.

Lemon Curd Fruit Tarts

1 RECIPE SUGAR TART DOUGH OR NUTTY CRUST
1 CUP GRANULATED SUGAR
GRATED ZEST OF LEMON
½ CUP FRESH-SQUEEZED LEMON JUICE
4 WHOLE EGGS
1 EGG YOLK
10 TABLESPOONS UNSALTED BUTTER
A HANDFUL OF GOOSEBERRIES, BLACKBERRIES,
   OR RASPBERRIES

Elegant little tarts for little hands or for "fancy" card parties and grange meetings.

For the lemon curd, mix the sugar and lemon zest together. Cut the butter into 1" pieces. In a nonreactive, heavy saucepan, combine the lemon juice, eggs, egg yolks, butter, and the lemon-sugar mixture. Over medium heat cook the mixture, stirring constantly, until it is thickened (4–5 minutes). Remove the pan from the heat before the mixture comes to a boil. Pour through a sieve into a bowl. Cover the top of the curd with a piece of plastic wrap to prevent a skin from forming.
Lemon Curd can be prepared ahead and frozen for up to three months.

Roll dough out to ¼" thickness. Place the dough over tart molds and gently press it into the molds with a bit of flour on your fingertips. Trim the dough by rolling the top of the tart molds with a rolling pin. Press the dough into the shells again for a perfect fit. Refrigerate the shells for at least 30 minutes. Preheat oven to 400 degrees. Prepare the molds for blind baking (see page 35). Bake the lined shells for 8 minutes. Remove the foil liners and bake the empty shells for a few more minutes, or until the pastry is a light golden brown. Cool. Remove from the molds. To finish the tarts, fill with lemon curd and top with gooseberries, blackberries, or raspberries.

Makes 8 3" tarts.

TASTY COBBLERS

There's nothing subtle about a cobbler. Nothing too fancy either. Basically it's the fusion of pie filling and crust baked in a deep oven dish and served warm (preferably with ice cream). They're a deep-dish, dig-in treat for those times when a pie crust isn't in the foreseeable future! I guarantee that nobody will complain when you bring it to the table.

The recipes that follow are but a sampling, and it is very easy to improvise off of these foundations. Cobblers are no frills and heavy on improvisation, and as a result, may be the key to unlocking some wonderful blend of fruit and spices that can be turned into your next blue ribbon pie!

Speedy Black Raspberry Cobbler

Success starts with **INGREDIENTS**

1 QUART BLACK RASPBERRIES
½ CUP SUGAR
2 TABLESPOONS FLOUR
1 TABLESPOON LEMON JUICE
1 CUP ALL-PURPOSE FLOUR
½ TEASPOON SALT
1 ¼ TEASPOONS BAKING POWDER
¼ CUP SHORTENING
½ CUP MILK MINUS 1 TABLESPOON

Super good and super fast! Easy to make and serve in a pinch—at least during berry season!

Preheat oven to 450 degrees.

Wash and drain fruit. Combine sugar and 2 tablespoons flour, and mix with berries. Add lemon juice and turn into buttered deep pie dish. Sift flour, measure, and resift with salt and baking powder. Cut in shortening with a pastry blender or two knives, and add milk all at once, stirring with a fork until dough clings together. Pat or roll out dough to ¼" thickness and place it on top of the fruit mixture. Trim edges and cut a design in the center for steam to escape. Bake at 450 degrees for 15 minutes. Reduce heat to 325 degrees and continue baking until berries are cooked through (about 20 minutes).

Serves 4.

Two-Fruit Orchard Cobbler

1 ½ CUP FLOUR
1 ½ TEASPOON BAKING POWDER
1 TABLESPOON SUGAR
¼ TEASPOON SALT
¼ CUP SHORTENING
1 EGG, SLIGHTLY BEATEN
¼ CUP MILK
1 ½ CUPS CHERRY PURÉE
1 LARGE APPLE, SLICED
¼ CUP SUGAR

Good old red sour cherry purée (or pie filling) combined with tart apples make this a rosy red and super sweet dessert or picnic special.

Preheat oven to 400 degrees.

Sift together the flour, baking powder, 1 tablespoon sugar, and salt. Cut in the shortening. Combine the egg and the milk in a bowl; add to flour mixture.

Knead 30 seconds on a floured board. Pat to fit on top of a 8 x 8 x 2" dish.

Combine cherry purée, apple, and ¼ cup sugar. Turn into baking dish, cover with the dough, and bake at 400 degrees for 25–30 minutes. Serve warm.

Serves 4.

Georgia Peach Cobbler

1 RECIPE OF SUGAR TART PASTRY DOUGH
2½ POUNDS RIPE, JUICY PEACHES [ABOUT 4 CUPS SLICED]
¾ CUP SUGAR
4 DROPS ALMOND EXTRACT
2 TABLESPOONS BUTTER

Easy as a peach! A great way to use those peaches getting too close to the end.

Preheat oven to 450 degrees. Peel peaches, or dip into boiling water for about a minute, and then slip off skins. Slice in eighths, discarding pit. Place in a shallow 6-cup baking dish or casserole, sprinkle with sugar and almond extract. Dot with butter. Roll pastry to fit top of baking dish and cut in any desired design for steam vents. Cover peaches with crust. Trim excess, turn under, let rest 10 minutes, then flute edge. Bake in a 450 degree oven for 15 minutes, then reduce to 325 degrees and bake 10 to 15 minutes or until peaches are cooked.

Serves 4.

Blackberry Cobbler

1 RECIPE OF SUGAR TART PASTRY DOUGH
½ CUP SUGAR
1 TABLESPOON FLOUR
1 QUART BLACKBERRIES, JUST RIPE

Deep and rich, perfect for family reunions and church socials.

Preheat oven to 450 degrees.

Divide dough in half. Line a 10" round shallow casserole, or a 7 x 11 x 2" baking pan, with pastry rolled out about ⅛" thick. Mix sugar and flour, and sprinkle half the mixture over the bottom pastry. Turn in washed, drained berries. Sift the rest of the sugar-flour mixture over the top. Roll out pastry for top crust to fit the dish. Cut a design for venting, lay the crust over the berries, and trim, or cut pastry for top crust into smaller, fancy-shaped pieces, one to a serving, and lay it over top. Let set for 10 minutes. Bake in a 450 degree oven for 15 minutes or until pastry is golden brown; then reduce heat to 325 degrees until berries are cooked through, about 20 minutes.

Serves 4.